Thank you for reading our American Heritage Songbook. We created the Heritage Songbook Series to promote musical understanding between children, parents, and educators around the world.

We hope you spend many happy hours with the children in your care singing these songs and listening to the accompanying recordings on Spotify, Amazon, Apple music, and Bandcamp.

We've also included color-coded sheet music so young instrumentalists can play and sing along. We recommend using colored rainbow bells or glockenspiels that match up with our notation system, but you can also use colored stickers on piano keys or ukulele frets if you would like.

Happy Music-Making!

From the Fiddlefox

www.fiddlefoxmusic.com

TABLE OF CONTENTS

AMERICAN HERITAGE SONGBOOK

Fiddlefox

HELLO FROM THE UNITED STATES!

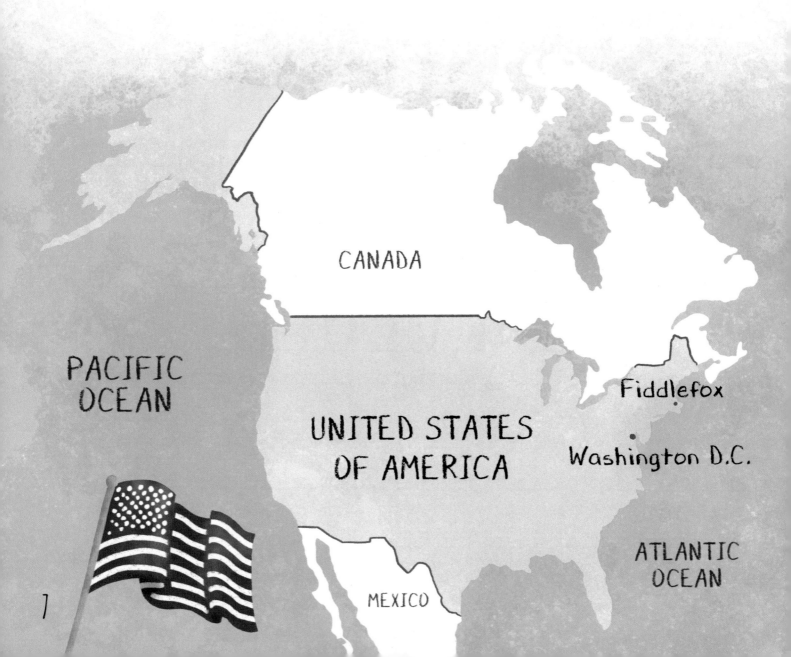

CANADA

PACIFIC
OCEAN

UNITED STATES
OF AMERICA

Fiddlefox

Washington D.C.

ATLANTIC
OCEAN

MEXICO

7

The USA is the third largest country in the world, and stretches across the North American continent. In the US you'll find frozen tundras, crystal lakes, dry deserts, tall mountains, murky swamps, and flat grassy plains, all inhabited by many species of animals and plants.

Founded in 1776, the United States of America is one of the world's great nations. With the exception of the Native Americans who lived there for thousands of years, most American citizens or their ancestors came to the USA in the last 300 years. The country is known as a "melting pot" where people from all over the world can come for life, liberty, and the pursuit of happiness.

The USA is also a melting pot of music, bringing new types of music to life that are enjoyed all over the world. This book takes four traditional American songs and reimagines them in four uniquely American music styles: Jazz, Hip Hop, Rock and Roll, and Country Western.

Welcome!.

SHE'LL BE COMING 'ROUND THE MOUNTAIN

SHE'LL BE COMING 'ROUND
THE MOUNTAIN
WHEN SHE COMES (2X)

9

SHE'LL BE COMING 'ROUND THE MOUNTAIN (2X)

SHE'LL BE COMING 'ROUND THE MOUNTAIN WHEN SHE COMES

SHE'LL BE DRIVING SIX WHITE HORSES
WHEN SHE COMES

SHE'LL BE DRIVING
SIX WHITE HORSES (2x)

12

SHE'LL BE WEARING PINK PAJAMAS
WHEN SHE COMES (2X)

SHE'LL BE WEARING
PINK PAJAMAS (2x)

SHE'LL BE WEARING
PINK PAJAMAS
WHEN SHE COMES

SHE'LL BE DRINKING SOUP
WITH DUMPLINGS (2x)

SHE'LL BE DRINKING SOUP
WITH DUMPLINGS
WHEN SHE COMES

16

SHE'LL BE COMING 'ROUND THE MOUNTAIN
WHEN SHE COMES (2X)

SHE'LL BE COMING 'ROUND
THE MOUNTAIN (2X)

SHE'LL BE COMING 'ROUND
THE MOUNTAIN
WHEN SHE COMES

SHE'LL BE COMING 'ROUND THE MOUNTAIN

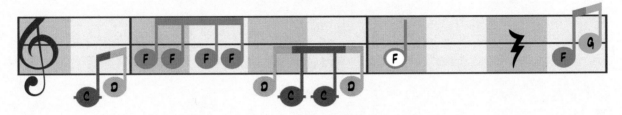

She'll be com-ing 'round the moun-tain when she comes.   She'll be

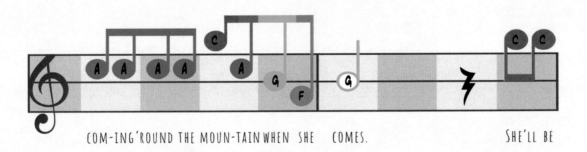

com-ing 'round the moun-tain when she   comes.   She'll be

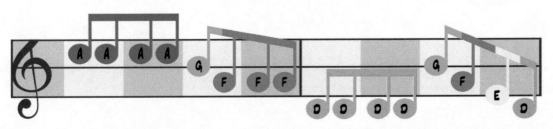

com-ing 'round the moun-tain she'll be com-ing 'round the moun-tain she'll be

21

JENNY JENKINS

WILL YOU WEAR RED, OH MY DEAR, OH MY DEAR
WILL YOU WEAR RED, JENNY JENKINS?

No, I won't wear red,
I'll stay in bed
I'll find me a
foldy roldy tildy toldy
seek a-double use-a-cuzza roll
to find me
Roll, Jenny Jenkins, roll

WILL YOU WEAR BLUE, OH MY DEAR, OH MY DEAR
WILL YOU WEAR BLUE, JENNY JENKINS?

No, I won't wear blue,
it just won't do
I'll find me a
foldy roldy tildy toldy
seek a-double use-a-cuzza roll
to find me
Roll, Jenny Jenkins, roll

WILL YOU WEAR GREEN, OH MY DEAR, OH MY DEAR
WILL YOU WEAR GREEN, JENNY JENKINS?

No, I won't wear green,
it's the color of a bean
I'll find me a
foldy roldy tildy toldy
seek a-double use-a-cuzza roll
to find me
Roll, Jenny Jenkins, roll

No, I won't wear pink,
it's the color of my sink
I'll find me a
foldy roldy tildy toldy
seek a-double use-a-cuzza roll
to find me
Roll, Jenny Jenkins, roll

30

WILL YOU WEAR WHITE, OH MY DEAR, OH MY DEAR
WILL YOU WEAR WHITE, JENNY JENKINS?

No, I won't wear white
It's far too bright
I'll find me a
Foldy roldy tildy toldy
Seek a-double use-a-cuzza roll
To find me
Roll, Jenny Jenkins, roll

WILL YOU WEAR ORANGE, OH MY DEAR, OH MY DEAR
WILL YOU WEAR ORANGE, JENNY JENKINS?

No, I won't wear orange,
'cause nothing rhymes with orange
I'll find me a
foldy roldy tildy toldy
seek a-double use-a-cuzza roll
to find me
Roll, Jenny Jenkins, roll

AMERICAN TRADITIONAL

JENNY JENKINS

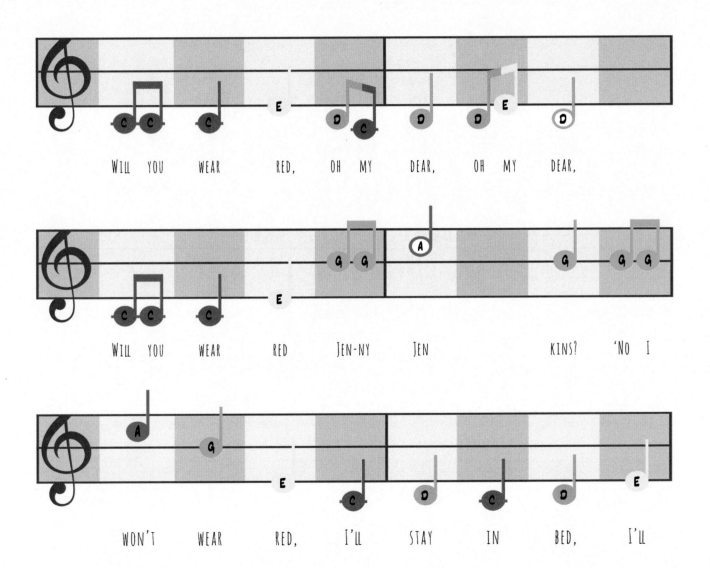

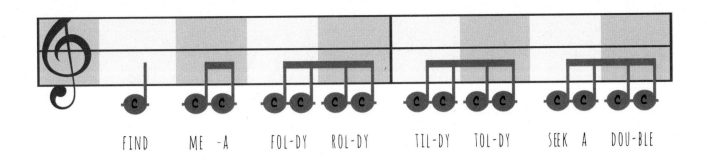

FIND   ME -A   FOL-DY   ROL-DY   TIL-DY   TOL-DY   SEEK A   DOU-BLE

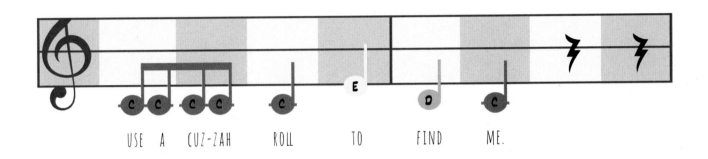

USE A   CUZ-ZAH   ROLL   TO   FIND   ME.

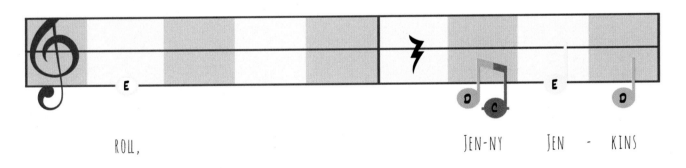

ROLL,   JEN-NY   JEN - KINS

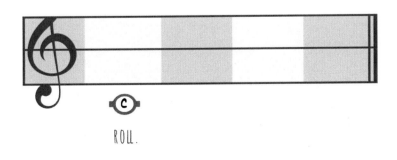

ROLL.

36

THE GREEN GRASS GROWS

THERE WAS A HOLE
DOWN IN THE GROUND
THE PRETTIEST HOLE
THAT YOU EVER DID SEE

WELL, THE HOLE IS
IN THE GROUND
AND THE GREEN GRASS
GROWS ALL AROUND

AND IN THE HOLE
THERE WAS A TREE
THE PRETTIEST TREE
THAT YOU EVER DID SEE

WELL, THE TREE IS IN THE
HOLE AND THE HOLE IS IN THE
GROUND AND THE GREEN
GRASS GROWS
ALL AROUND

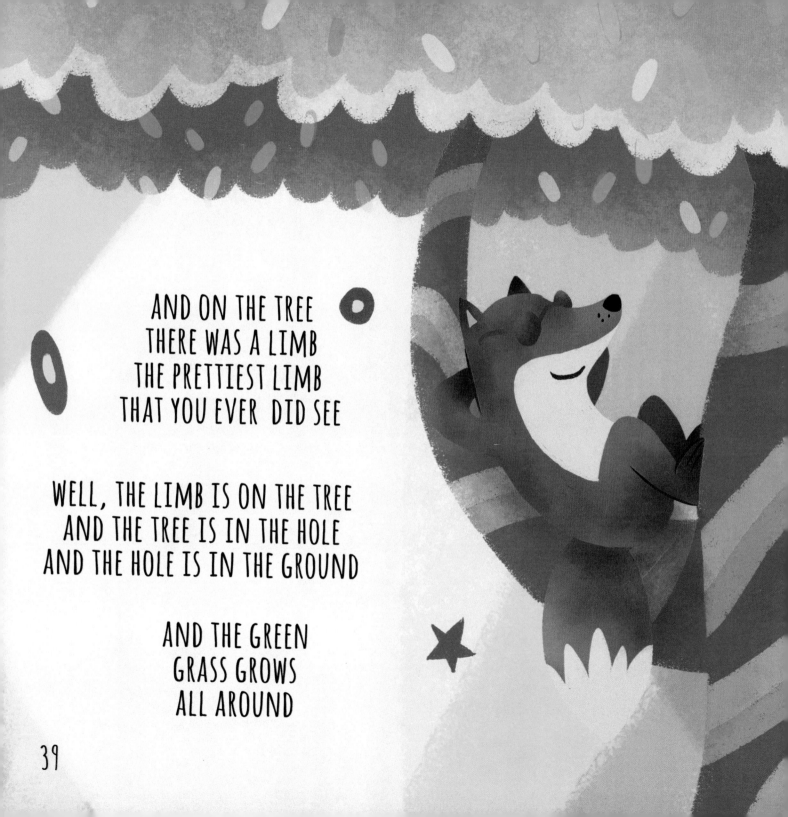

AND ON THE TREE
THERE WAS A LIMB
THE PRETTIEST LIMB
THAT YOU EVER DID SEE

WELL, THE LIMB IS ON THE TREE
AND THE TREE IS IN THE HOLE
AND THE HOLE IS IN THE GROUND

AND THE GREEN
GRASS GROWS
ALL AROUND

AND ON THE LIMB
THERE WAS A BRANCH
THE PRETTIEST BRANCH
THAT YOU EVER DID SEE

WELL, THE BRANCH IS ON THE LIMB
AND THE LIMB IS ON THE TREE
AND THE TREE IS IN THE HOLE
AND THE HOLE IS IN THE GROUND

AND THE GREEN
GRASS GROWS
ALL AROUND

40

AND ON THE BRANCH
THERE WAS A LEAF
THE PRETTIEST LEAF
THAT YOU EVER DID SEE

WELL, THE LEAF IS ON THE BRANCH
AND THE BRANCH IS ON THE LIMB
AND THE LIMB IS ON THE TREE
AND THE TREE IS IN THE HOLE
AND THE HOLE IS IN THE GROUND

AND THE GREEN
GRASS GROWS
ALL AROUND

41

AND ON THE LEAF
THERE WAS A NEST
THE PRETTIEST NEST
THAT YOU EVER DID SEE

WELL, THE NEST IS ON THE LEAF
AND THE LEAF IS ON THE BRANCH
AND THE BRANCH IS ON THE LIMB
AND THE LIMB IS ON THE TREE
AND TREE IS IN THE HOLE
AND THE HOLE IS IN THE GROUND

AND THE GREEN
GRASS GROWS
ALL AROUND

42

AND IN THE NEST
THERE WAS AN EGG
THE PRETTIEST EGG
THAT YOU EVER DID SEE

WELL THE EGG IS IN THE NEST
AND THE NEST IS ON THE LEAF
AND THE LEAF IS ON THE BRANCH
AND THE BRANCH IS ON THE LIMB

AND THE LIMB IS ON THE TREE
AND THE TREE IS IN THE HOLE
AND THE HOLE IS IN THE GROUND

AND THE GREEN
GRASS GROWS
ALL AROUND

WELL THE BIRD IS IN THE EGG
AND THE EGG IS IN THE NEST
AND THE NEST IS ON THE LEAF
AND THE LEAF IS ON THE BRANCH
AND THE BRANCH IS ON THE LIMB
AND THE LIMB IS ON THE TREE
AND THE TREE IS IN THE HOLE
AND THE HOLE IS IN THE GROUND
AND THE GREEN GRASS GROWS
ALL AROUND

THE GREEN GRASS GROWS

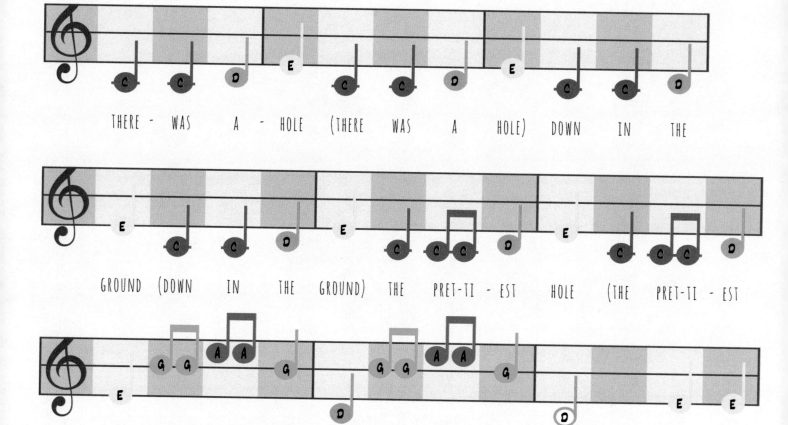

47

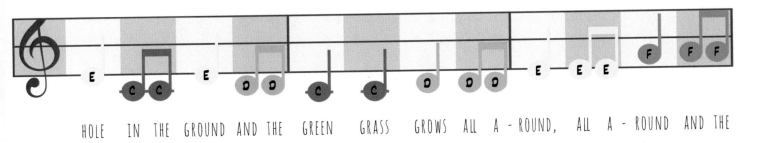

HOLE IN THE GROUND AND THE GREEN GRASS GROWS ALL A - ROUND, ALL A - ROUND AND THE

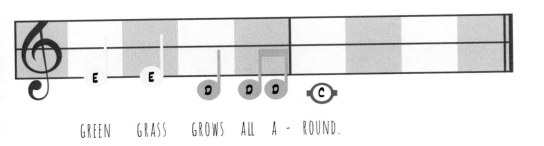

GREEN GRASS GROWS ALL A - ROUND.

HOME ON THE RANGE

OH, GIVE ME A HOME
WHERE THE BUFFALO ROAM
WHERE THE DEER
AND THE ANTELOPE PLAY

49

WHERE SELDOM IS HEARD
A DISCOURAGING WORD
AND THE SKIES ARE NOT
CLOUDY ALL DAY

50

HOME!
HOME ON THE RANGE!
WHERE THE DEER
AND THE ANTELOPE PLAY

OH, GIVE ME THE GLEAM
OF A SWIFT MOUNTAIN STREAM
AND A PLACE WHERE
NO HURRICANE BLOWS

OH, GIVE ME A PARK
WHERE THE PRAIRIE DOGS BARK
AND THE MOUNTAIN
IS COVERED WITH SNOW

HOME!
HOME ON THE RANGE!
WHERE THE DEER
AND THE ANTELOPE PLAY

OH, GIVE ME
A LAND
WHERE THE BRIGHT
DIAMOND SAND
FLOWS IN A
LEISURELY STREAM

57

WHERE THE
GRACEFUL WHITE SWAN
GOES A-GLIDING ALONG
LIKE A MAID IN
A HEAVENLY DREAM

58

HOME!
HOME ON THE RANGE!
WHERE THE DEER
AND THE ANTELOPE PLAY

WHERE SELDOM IS HEARD
A DISCOURAGING WORD
AND THE SKIES ARE NOT
CLOUDY ALL DAY

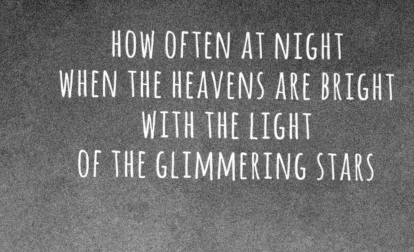

HOW OFTEN AT NIGHT
WHEN THE HEAVENS ARE BRIGHT
WITH THE LIGHT
OF THE GLIMMERING STARS

Have I stood here amazed
and I asked as I gazed
"Is somebody out staring at ours?"

HOME!
HOME ON THE RANGE!
WHERE THE DEER
AND THE ANTELOPE PLAY

WHERE SELDOM IS HEARD
A DISCOURAGING WORD
AND THE SKIES ARE NOT
CLOUDY ALL DAY

64

HOME ON THE RANGE

BRING A WORLD OF MUSIC HOME WITH
FIDDLEFOX WORLD HERITAGE SONGBOOKS!

GAMBIAN HERITAGE
SONGBOOK

RUSSIAN HERITAGE
SONGBOOK

TURKISH HERITAGE
SONGBOOK

CHINESE HERITAGE
SONGBOOK

Journey around the world with Fiddlefox World Heritage Storybooks!

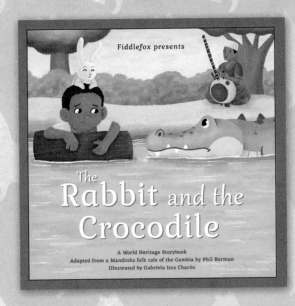

Fiddlefox presents

The Rabbit and the Crocodile

A World Heritage Storybook
Adapted from a Mandinka folk tale of the Gambia by Phil Berman
Illustrated by Gabriela Issa Chacón

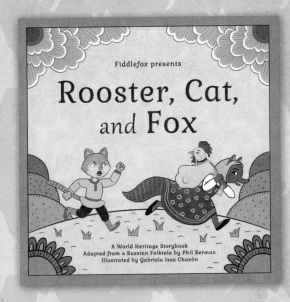

Fiddlefox presents

Rooster, Cat, and Fox

A World Heritage Storybook
Adapted from a Russian Folktale by Phil Berman
Illustrated by Gabriela Issa Chacón

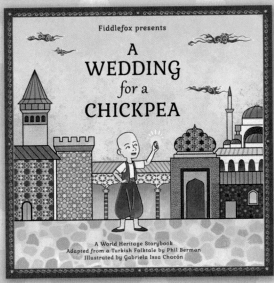

Fiddlefox presents

A WEDDING for a CHICKPEA

A World Heritage Storybook
Adapted from a Turkish Folktale by Phil Berman
Illustrated by Gabriela Issa Chacón

Fiddlefox presents

The Dragon's Pearl

A World Heritage Storybook
Adapted from a Sichuan folktale of China by Phil Berman
Illustrated by Gabriela Issa Chacón

Available on iBooks and Amazon!
www.fiddlefoxmusic.com

Made in the USA
Middletown, DE
10 June 2021

41692199R00040